ALTERNATOR BOOKS™

SPACE IN ACTION

PLANETS IN ACTION

An AUGMENTED REALITY Experience

Rebecca E. Hirsch

Lerner Publications ◆ Minneapolis

EXPLORE SPACE IN BRAND-NEW WAYS WITH AUGMENTED REALITY!

1. Ask a parent or guardian for permission to download the free Lerner AR app on your digital device by going to the App Store or Google Play.

2. As you read, look for this icon throughout the book. It means there is an augmented reality experience on that page!

3. Use the Lerner AR app to scan the picture near the icon.

4. Watch space come alive with augmented reality!

CONTENTS

INTRODUCTION
ALIEN LANDING

On November 26, 2018, the *InSight* spacecraft pierced the **atmosphere** around Mars and flew through the thin air at about 14,000 miles (22,530 km) an hour. Out popped a parachute to slow the spacecraft. The heat shield dropped off. Then *InSight* touched down on the cold, dusty planet and began to search for clues to how rocky planets form.

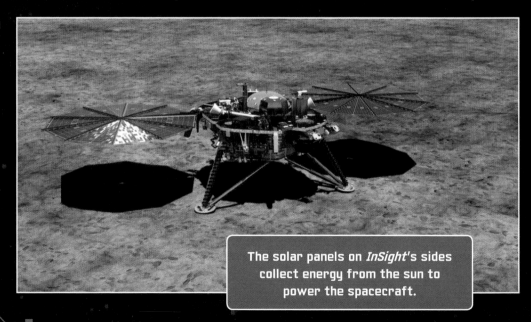

The solar panels on *InSight*'s sides collect energy from the sun to power the spacecraft.

The solar system has an asteroid belt,
a region of rocky objects, between the
orbits of Mars and Jupiter.

Eight planets travel around the sun. Mercury, Venus, Earth, and Mars are the inner planets. They are smaller than the other planets in the **solar system**, and they have a rocky surface. The outer planets are Jupiter, Saturn, Uranus, and Neptune. They are giants and made mostly of swirling gases. Beyond the outer planets lie **dwarf planets** and other icy objects in a region astronomers call the Kuiper Belt. These objects also **orbit** the blazing sun.

CHAPTER 1

MERCURY AND VENUS

From Mercury, the sun appears as a huge fiery ball in the sky. Mercury is the closest planet to the sun and the smallest planet in the solar system. It is only a little bigger than Earth's moon. Mercury has a rocky surface with many **craters** and little air. During the day, the temperature can reach 800°F (427°C). At night, it might drop to −290°F (−179°C).

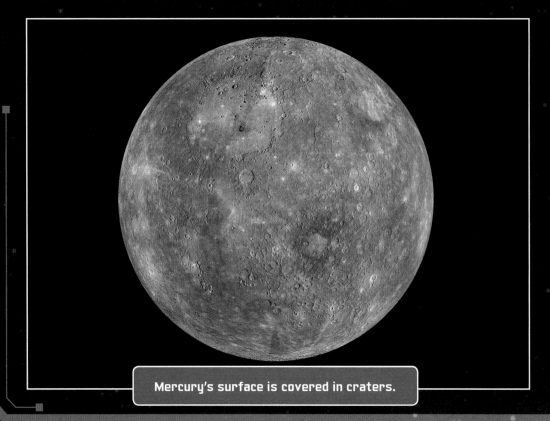

Mercury's surface is covered in craters.

Only two spacecraft have visited Mercury: *Mariner 10* from 1974 to 1975 and *MESSENGER* from 2011 to 2015. The newest mission to Mercury, BepiColombo, blasted off in 2018. Two spacecraft from the mission will enter the planet's orbit in 2025 to study its **geology** and atmosphere.

HOT, CLOUDY VENUS

Venus is the second planet from the sun and about the same size as Earth. Like Mercury, Venus has no moons. The rocky surface of Venus has mountains, plains, and volcanoes. Its thick atmosphere is full of carbon dioxide and clouds of **sulfuric acid**.

Venus has the hottest surface temperature of any planet in the solar system.

Venus is scorching hot thanks to its thick atmosphere. Sunlight heats the planet's surface, and the atmosphere traps the heat. The surface of Venus is a toasty 880°F (471°C). That's hot enough to melt lead!

More than forty spacecraft have explored Venus. The latest is *Akatsuki* from Japan. It is orbiting the planet, searching to see if Venus has lightning in the clouds or active volcanoes on the surface.

CHAPTER 2

eaRTH anD THe MOON

On January 2, 2019, China's *Chang'e-4* lander touched down on Earth's moon to study its geology. A **rover** emerged and rolled down a ramp. Its wheels left tracks in the cold, gray dirt. Because the moon has no water and little air to **erode** the land, the tracks may last for millions of years.

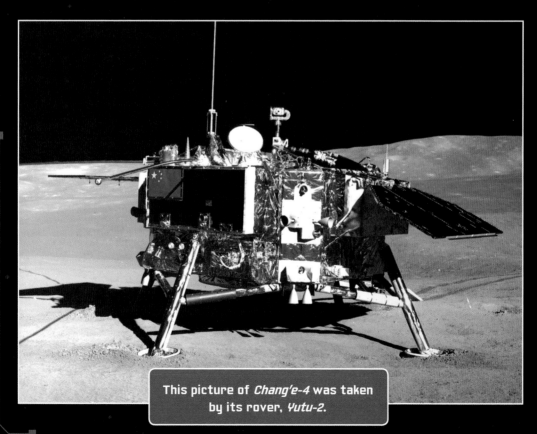

This picture of *Chang'e-4* was taken by its rover, *Yutu-2*.

JUST RIGHT FOR LIFE

Earth, the third planet from the sun, is the only planet in the solar system with liquid water on its surface. It is also the only planet with living things, as far as we know. Liquid water is important to life as we know it. Earth's location 93 million miles (150 million km) from the sun makes it just right for liquid water. If Earth were closer, the water would boil away. If it were farther from the sun, the water would freeze.

Earth's atmosphere protects it from many incoming **meteoroids**. They burn up in the atmosphere before they can reach the surface. A large meteoroid that reaches Earth's surface is a meteorite.

Earth is the most explored planet in the solar system, yet we're still learning more. Many satellites orbit Earth, and some study our planet's weather. For example, when Hurricane Michael formed in the Atlantic Ocean in 2018, satellites helped scientists predict the storm's path.

Satellite images such as this one helped scientists determine where and when Hurricane Michael would reach land.

THE MOON

Earth has one moon. Long ago, the moon had active volcanoes, but they haven't erupted for millions of years.

The side of the moon you can see from Earth is always the same side. It is mostly flat with few craters, but the far side of the moon looks different. Craters cover it. With a thin atmosphere, the moon is not protected from objects hitting it. Why one side of the moon has more craters than the other is a mystery.

The moon's gravity causes predictable rises and falls in the surface of the sea on Earth called tides.

The moon is the only part of the solar system outside of Earth that people have visited. American astronauts went there in the 1960s and 1970s. Twelve astronauts walked on the moon, all on the near side. No other country has sent people to the moon, but several robotic missions have explored it in recent years. NASA's Lunar Reconnaissance Orbiter orbits the moon and studies its dusty surface.

NASA astronaut Charles M. Duke Jr. collects rock and dust samples on the moon during the Apollo 16 mission in 1972.

In 2019 the *Chang'e-4* lander released the *Yutu-2* rover on the far side of the moon. The rover began rolling around, photographing the terrain, and analyzing the soil. The mission may solve some of the mysteries of the moon, such as why the near and far sides look so different. Learning more about the moon might help future astronauts visit its far side.

Earth's moon orbits about 239,000 miles (385,000 km) above the planet's surface.

CHAPTER 3

MARS

I n 2018 an instrument on the *InSight* lander picked up a low rumble on Mars. It was no earthly sound. The instrument had recorded the howl of Martian winds blowing across the dusty planet.

This illustration shows *InSight* digging into the Martian soil to explore the planet's interior temperature.

Mars is mostly red except for the two poles, where frozen water makes them white.

Mars's nickname is the Red Planet. The color comes from the planet's rusty-red-colored soil and dust. It has two small moons, Phobos and Deimos. Like Earth, Mars has volcanoes, canyons, and polar **ice caps** full of frozen water. But it has a thin atmosphere and is colder than Earth. The average temperature on Mars is −80°F (−62°C).

LOOKING FOR LIFE ON MARS

Mars may have been warmer and wetter billions of years ago with rivers, oceans, and a thicker atmosphere. Scientists want to know if Mars once had tiny living things called **microorganisms**. They also want to know if Mars can support life.

The *Curiosity* rover is about the size of an average car.

The uneven surface of Mars is a challenge for rovers to navigate.

Humans have sent many missions to the planet to search for evidence of life. Orbiters in space around Mars map its surface and study its atmosphere. In 2018 an orbiter detected a salty underground lake that might support life. Rovers on the surface have snapped photographs and examined the planet's rocks and soil. Since 2012 NASA's *Curiosity* rover has studied the planet and found conditions that may be suitable for microorganisms.

NASA's *InSight* lander is investigating under the surface of Mars. One instrument is measuring underground heat. Another is listening for **marsquakes**. This information may help scientists discover how Mars and other rocky planets change over time.

More spaceships are destined for the Red Planet. They will continue the search for signs of alien life and will study how people might live and work on Mars in the future. These missions will test how to make oxygen from the Martian atmosphere and how weather, dust, and other conditions could affect future astronauts.

This helicopter, which will launch on a mission to Mars in 2020, could become the first flying robotic explorer on the planet's surface.

Orion will be able to take astronauts farther into space than ever before and return them safely to Earth.

Someday it may be safe for people to explore Mars. Orion is a new NASA spacecraft designed to carry people and cargo deep into space. It may someday carry the first human explorers to Mars.

THE OUTER PLANETS

The outer planets are giant, alien worlds of swirling gases and liquids. They make Earth look like a calm, tiny place.

Jupiter is about one thousand times larger than Earth.

THE GAS GIANTS

The biggest planet in the solar system is Jupiter. It has four large moons and many smaller moons. On its surface swirls the Great Red Spot, a giant, spinning storm that is wider than Earth. Jupiter is covered by cold clouds, their temperature dipping to about −234°F (−148°C). Deep under the clouds, Jupiter's core is very hot. It may be hotter than the surface of the sun.

NASA's *Juno* spacecraft is studying Jupiter from orbit. It is searching for clues to how the giant formed and evolved.

Juno launched from Earth in 2011 and arrived at Jupiter in 2016.

Jupiter cannot support life as we know it, but its moon Europa holds an ocean beneath its icy surface. Scientists think this ocean might have the right conditions for life. NASA scientists and engineers hope to send a lander to Europa to search for signs of life.

Like Jupiter, Saturn is a giant ball of gas. It has beautiful rings spinning around it that contain chunks of ice and rock. Saturn has more than sixty moons of different shapes and sizes. From 2004 to 2017, the *Cassini* spacecraft studied Saturn. It wove among the planet's rings and moons and sent detailed pictures back to Earth.

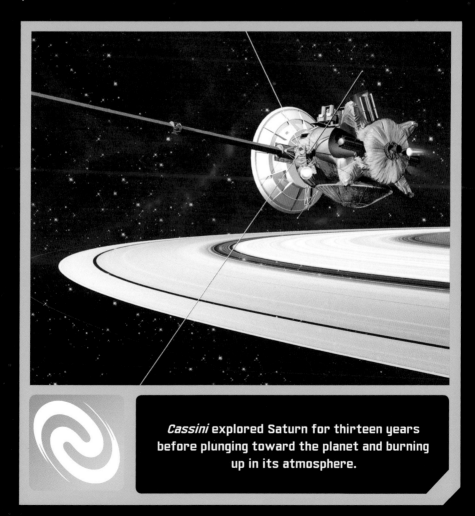

Cassini explored Saturn for thirteen years before plunging toward the planet and burning up in its atmosphere.

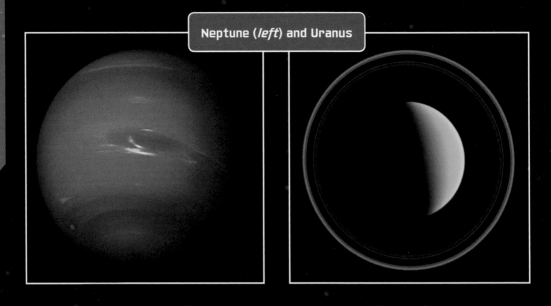

Neptune (*left*) and Uranus

The seventh and eighth planets, Uranus and Neptune, are made of gas and liquid around a small, rocky core. Uranus has faint rings and twenty-seven moons. Neptune has more than a dozen moons. It has winds that howl at speeds of more than 1,200 miles (1,931 km) per hour.

THE DWARF PLANETS

Farther out in the solar system are many dwarf planets in the Kuiper Belt. Pluto, the most famous of these, used to be called the ninth planet, but in 2006 astronomers agreed to change its status to dwarf planet. Pluto is smaller than Earth's moon. In recent decades, astronomers have discovered many Pluto-size objects in the Kuiper Belt. *New Horizons* spacecraft sailed past Pluto in 2015 and took the first close-up images of this mysterious dwarf planet.

Astronomers think another unseen planet may exist far past Pluto. Who knows what planetary discoveries are awaiting astronomers in our solar system?

It took *New Horizons* almost nine years to reach Pluto.

Follow the links below to download 3D printer files for some of the space exploration vehicles in this book.

Lunar Reconnaissance Orbiter: http://qrs.lernerbooks.com/LRO

Orion: http://qrs.lernerbooks.com/Orion

Cassini: http://qrs.lernerbooks.com/Cassini

Juno: http://qrs.lernerbooks.com/Juno

atmosphere: gases surrounding a planet

craters: bowl-shaped holes on the ground made by the impact of an object, such as a meteorite

dwarf planets: round objects too small to be planets that orbit the sun with similar objects

erode: to wear away by the action of wind, water, or ice

geology: the study of a planet's solid material

ice caps: large sheets of ice that form on land

marsquakes: the trembling or shaking of Mars similar to earthquakes

meteoroids: small rocky objects from space

microorganisms: living things that are too small to be seen without a microscope

orbit: to move around a body in space, or the path around that body

rover: a wheeled, robotic machine used for exploring the ground of a planet or moon

solar system: the sun and everything that orbits it, including planets and dwarf planets

sulfuric acid: a strong acid that eats away at many solid substances

Beth, Georgia. *Discover Mars*. Minneapolis: Lerner Publications, 2018.

Kenney, Karen Latchana. *Breakthroughs in Planet and Comet Research*. Minneapolis: Lerner Publications, 2019.

Kopp, Megan. *Unlocking the Secrets of the Solar System*. New York: Crabtree, 2019.

NASA: Mars for Kids
https://mars.jpl.nasa.gov/participate/funzone/

NASA Space Place: All about Pluto
https://spaceplace.nasa.gov/ice-dwarf/en/

NASA Space Place: Solar System
https://spaceplace.nasa.gov/menu/solar-system/

National Geographic Kids: Mission to Venus
https://kids.nationalgeographic.com/explore/space/mission-to
-venus/#venus-planet.jpg

Sommer, Nathan. *Pluto & the Dwarf Planets*. Minneapolis: Bellwether Media, 2019.

Photo Acknowledgments

Image credits: Freer/Shutterstock.com, p. 2 (bottom); NASA, pp. 4, 11, 12, 14, 21, 22; Laura Westlund/Independent Picture Service, p. 5; NASA/Johns Hopkins University Applied Physics Laboratory/Carnegie Institution of Washington, pp. 6, 7; NASA/JPL, pp. 8; 26 (left); JAXA, p. 9; CNSA via CNS/AFP/Getty Images, p. 10; Bill Oxford/Getty Images, p. 13; Ramberg/Getty Images, p. 15; NASA/JPL-Caltech, pp. 16, 18, 19, 20, 23, 25; ESA & MPS for OSIRIS Team MPS/UPD/LAM/IAA/RSSD /INTA/UPM/DASP/IDA, p. 17; NASA/JPL-Caltech/SETI Institute, p. 24; SCIEPRO /Getty Images, p. 26 (right); NASA/JHUAPL/SwRI, p. 27; NASA, ESA, A. Simon (GSFC) and the OPAL Team, and J. DePasquale (STScI), p. 28. Design elements: Jetrel/Shutterstock.com; Nanashiro/Shutterstock.com; phiseksit/Shutterstock. com; MSSA/Shutterstock.com; Pakpoom Makpan/Shutterstock.com; pixelparticle /Shutterstock.com; wacomka/Shutterstock.com; fluidworkshop/Shutterstock.com.

Cover: mozzyb/Shutterstock.com.

Lerner Publications Company
An imprint of Lerner Publishing Group, Inc.
241 First Avenue North
Minneapolis, MN USA 55401

For reading levels and more information, look up this title at www.lernerbooks.com.

Main body text set in Aptifer Sans LT Pro.
Typeface provided by Linotype AG.

Library of Congress Cataloging-in-Publication Data

Names: Hirsch, Rebecca E., author.
Title: Planets in action : an augmented reality experience / Rebecca E. Hirsch.
Description: Minneapolis : Lerner Publications, [2020] | Series: Space in action (Alternator books) | Audience: Ages 8–12. | Audience: Grades 4 to 6. | Includes bibliographical references and index.
Identifiers: LCCN 2019010623 (print) | LCCN 2019014073 (ebook) | ISBN 9781541583481 (eb pdf) | ISBN 9781541578784 (lb : alk. paper)
Subjects: LCSH: Planets—Juvenile literature. | Outer planets—Juvenile literature. | Solar system—Juvenile literature.
Classification: LCC QB602 (ebook) | LCC QB602 .H57 2020 (print) | DDC 523.4—dc23

LC record available at https://lccn.loc.gov/2019010623

Manufactured in the United States of America
1-46981-47850-5/14/2019